Bugs, Floods, and Fried Rice

ONE MOM'S JOURNAL

Darlene Sala

BAKER BOOK HOUSE
Grand Rapids, Michigan

CONTENTS

PREFACE

The day Nancy was born in California, little did I think that her first day at school would be in the Philippines. Yet there she was, less than twelve hours after our plane landed in Manila, walking away at 6:20 a.m. for an hour-long bus ride to attend a school I had never seen.

I have to admit it was a little scary. At the same time I had a deep sense of God's guiding hand on our lives. And a prayer was in my heart that I would not waste any of the opportunity God was giving us to live for Him these two years in the Philippines.

Now, two years later, I'd like you to share our impressions and experiences. Perhaps you will wonder why these vignettes are not more organized. There is a reason—I didn't try to categorize them simply because they didn't happen in categories. Life comes to all of us as an everchanging mixture of the sublime and the ridiculous, the tragic and the glorious, not in neatly separated chapters but as quickly overlapping experiences. Actually the scenes are fairly chronological, and from them I hope you can catch a glimpse of "how it was."

1

OPEN MY EYES, LORD

One day in Manila, my husband Harold saw a little boy stretch his eyes vertically to make them look round—his counterpart to the way American kids stretch their eyes sideways to make them look oriental. Funny!

Lord, You've made us in all shapes and sizes and skin shades. Yet for all of us You are God. Open my eyes, Lord, to see the world a bit more as You see it. And help me never to forget that Jesus is the answer to its needs.

*"For if once I could see this world the way You see, I just know I'd serve You more faithfully"**

*From *Looking Through His Eyes* by Mike Otto

2

WHY HAVE YOU COME?

A successful insurance salesman came by to meet Harold. Like so many who presume we have lived in the Philippines for a long time because they have heard Harold on the radio for years, Frank Jiminez had no idea we had just come.

Harold was in a conference at the time, so I sat down to visit. One of Frank's first questions was, "Why have you come to the Philippines?" (asked in a tone of voice that implied, "Who would choose to leave the U.S. to come here?")

"Because we believe God has directed us here," I answered.

"I suppose people like you can get guidance from God," replied Frank. I was about to tell him about Proverbs 3:5 and 6 when Harold came in. The first thing he asked Harold was, "Why have you come here?"

What did Harold answer? "Because we feel God has sent us here and has a work for us to do."

Frank looked at me in surprise and said, "That's what your wife said too!"

FRUSTRATION!

I'm so glad we have enough space in our home for Harold's office and the little storeroom for a recording studio. With all this traffic and the rain he'd lose much time if he had to drive to an office.

But will he ever get that studio finished? The old air conditioner, frozen tight by rust and corrosion, had long since breathed its last and had to be chiseled out. The small new one we bought just before leaving the U.S. was defective and has to be rebuilt. A second air conditioner we brought was an inch too wide for the installation hole. Harold had to break out concrete to make room for it (for a month or so until the small one is repaired). Then he'll pull out the large one, install the small one, and fill in the extra space.

In the meantime, with no air conditioning, the acoustic tile he put up is sliding down the wall and the Flexowriter we have in the studio required a service call to get its keys unstuck.

I think today the devil is snickering.

4

INSECTS

Nancy is studying insects at school. She must be the most avid collector in her entire class. Her largest find so far has been a three and one-half-inch cockroach which she put in a jar. One morning as school started, her sister, Bonnie, who was on the second floor of another building, heard a scream that could only be Nancy's. She and the rest of her class ran to the window in time to see Nancy jumping up and down and pointing.

"Miss Lacey, Miss Lacey," she screamed, "my cockroach! Miss Lacey, my cockroach is going in the boys' bathroom!"

Into the boys' bathroom went Miss Lacey followed by a string of kindergarteners. Soon the cockroach was safely back in the jar. Nancy examined the jar closely. Another cry. "But Miss Lacey, where's my *caterpillar*?"

MONSOON

The word *monsoon* has graphic meaning to me now. It has rained hard for the past two weeks, which has caused much flooding. Many are homeless. One province is 90 percent under water. Harold's service this evening was canceled because there is water in the church building.

I have real admiration for the engineers of FEBC (Far East Broadcasting Company) who wade out in the rice paddies to make antenna repairs—in twelve inches of mud and hip-deep water! Having been here to see what it's like, I'm more apt to remember to pray for their safety as they make electrical repairs in all that water.

When it rains hard even for thirty minutes, some of the streets become flooded. Water pours off the corrugated metal roofs in waterfalls. Children—and even adults—like to stand under the downpour; as hot as the weather is, I can understand why.

Filipinos have a sense of humor that helps them through difficult circumstances. I watched a man wade through six inches of water at a gas station. When he saw I was watching, he was not embarrassed but broke into a big smile. Filipinos nearly always return a smile and are eager to make conversation. Very warm people—like their weather!

DARKNESS

It's fascinating to listen to people tell how God met them at their point of need during the horror of World War II. Take the Elegados, for instance. In his work for the copper and gold mines during the Japanese occupation of the Philippines, Mr. Elegado had the only car allowed to go back and forth to the mines near Baguio. In order to be permitted to pass check points he had to have a Japanese sticker on the car. Eventually, however, he was arrested by the Japanese and taken to Manila to prison.

For months his wife left their three children every weekend to search for her husband. Since she was a nurse, she knew that if she did not find him he would die, for he could not survive indefinitely on the daily ration of one bowl of rice and a lump of sugar or salt. Her heart cried out, "If there *is* a God—if You are really alive—help me find my husband."

At the end of eight months of searching, she found him and began to bring food to him. God preserved his life through two more years of imprisonment. Ever since that time she and her husband have been dedicated to doing all they can for the Lord who literally gave them back their lives.

There is a postscript to the story. The Japanese imprisonment, horrible as it was, saved Mr. Elegado's life. For immediately after he was arrested, the Filipino guerillas came through the area to kill him—the sticker on his car to them meant cooperation with the enemy.

When we are in a very dark place, perhaps the darkness is only the shadow of God's hand shielding us from greater danger.

7

"ALONG CAME A SPIDER"

Harold and I are speaking at a women's retreat two and one half hours from Manila. Ninety women are registered from a number of churches. This is nothing less than Tarzan country with banana trees, tall, tall bamboo, and even taller coconut palms. Vines hang there just waiting to be swung on. When it isn't raining, it's steaming. Beautiful greenery. Large red and black butterflies. At night, brilliant stars above the palms.

The cabins have wooden beds. Filipinos don't always use mattresses, but they gave us a room with a box spring which we covered with straw mats and then our sheets. As we were about to make the bed I noticed we had company—a speckled brown spider on the wall at least five inches in diameter. He met a quick death with Harold's tennis shoe. I wonder how long it will take for my insides to get used to living with bugs, especially big ones?

POVERTY

I once complimented a girl on how slender she was. Immediately I sensed I had said the wrong thing (something I did occasionally in a new culture!). Later I learned that being thin is equated with being poor.

Poverty is so prevalent—I wonder where Christian responsibility begins and ends. "What can *I* do amid such great need?" I give food to the beggar woman who comes to the door with her small son and baby. She asks for money "to get out of Manila to the province where there is food," yet my neighbor Judy Sutphen says she has been coming door-to-door for years. We both continue to give her food. I think she finds begging more profitable than work. But how do I know?

At a traffic light it is common for a child to lead a blind person over to the car to ask for money. Much of this is syndicated. They can make more money working for the "begging syndicate" than at a legitimate job. What really breaks one's heart (and they know it) is the sight of little children carrying around baby brothers and sisters while they beg. One night we had to walk around a baby sleeping on the bare sidewalk while her sister begged.

Since inflation has caused all prices to double or triple in the last two years, more people must be hungry. That is why one of the items people find stolen from their homes is *rice*. Though the government is fighting malnutrition, one out of every two Filipino children under age six dies of malnutrition or a related disease. The minimum wage is $1.25 a day. The average family has seven children.

A mainstay in the *barrios* (villages) is the *sari-sari* store, a kind of "corner store" that sells a bit of everything. They are independently owned and perform a needed service in the rural areas where people have no refrigeration and must buy from meal to meal. The majority of purchases run from five to fifty centavos (one-half cent to seven cents). There, instead of buying a stick of butter, you can buy one slice for fifteen centavos. Or you can buy three tablespoons of milk for ten centavos. I think of that when I put three pounds of margarine in the freezer and six cans of milk on the shelf. I realize I don't understand what it means to be poor.

MANILA TRAFFIC

Driving here is quite an experience. The Book of Judges describes it perfectly when it says, "Every man did that which was right in his own eyes." Whoever gets his bumper there first has the right of way. Drivers don't let their eyes meet, for that would mean conceding the right of way. Yet tempers seldom flare.

One evening we were to have dinner with four couples involved in tribal missionary work. Since we couldn't all fit in one car, some had to follow us to the restaurant in a taxi through downtown rush-hour traffic. After managing to stay up with us, the cab driver commented about Harold's driving, "He drives like a taxi driver! He must be from Southern California!"

If a car breaks down (and they often do) there's no need to push it over to the side of the road—just repair it right where it is. One evening as Mr. and Mrs. Fred Magbanua (director of FEBC Philippines), were taking us to dinner, Fred's car had a flat tire right in an underpass on the busiest thoroughfare in Manila. In true Filipino style he and Harold in their dress clothes changed the tire right where it happened—in the left-hand lane.

City driving never bores me here. The Western eye is caught by the sight of a huge, towering wagonload of baskets being pulled to market by a brahma bull, or a jeepney on the way to market with a butchered and skinned hog draped over its side. Fifty percent of all the jeeps the U.S. ever produced must be in Manila! Plus strings and string of buses.

The transportation here is fascinating. If you don't drive, you may choose from tricycle (motorcycle with elaborate sidecar), *calesa* (horse-drawn cart), *jeepney* (jeep with body brightly painted and modified to carry passengers), mini-bus, conventional bus or taxi—all for public hire and costing from three cents to one dollar.

I noticed once that there is no place on the application for driver's license to indicate color of hair or eyes. That information wouldn't help much in Asia!

10

INADEQUATE

September 1

Harold spoke at a large church in a rather poor area this morning. I didn't feel very zippy. The weather was hot, the acoustics bad, much of the service was in Tagalog, which I don't understand, the benches were hard, and I had a difficult time entering into worship because of all the things that were bothering me. I felt an overwhelming sense of inadequacy to communicate with people from an entirely different background—conversation is hard for me anyway.

Do I really love them, missing teeth and lice and all? Do I feel so superior to them that I'm unable to communicate? Today I just felt it was a waste of time and money and energy for me to even be here. Many of the women had beautiful smiles. I could see they loved the Lord very much and are happy in Jesus. But here I was so affected by the change in culture that it was all I could think of. Took a long nap and still awoke with a bad headache. Went to bed early feeling defeated.

September 2

Psalm 94:16: "Lord, when doubts fill my mind, when my heart is in turmoil, quiet me and give me renewed hope and cheer."

Praise God, He doesn't give up on us! We have bad days when our love reaches its limit, but God's love never fails. Instead of berating us for our shortcomings and stumblings, He picks us up, dusts us off, sets us on our feet again, and renews our strength for the tasks ahead. And today I am reassured that the tasks He gives will be suited to our capabilities.

11

APPRECIATION

"I even thank the Lord for this leprosy. I know the Lord knows what is best for me." Tears filled my eyes as I read this letter from a man who lives near Manila. He had written a few weeks ago asking for prayer. Harold wrote to him and sent him our booklet "Guidelines for Peace of Mind." Today his letter tells us he has accepted Christ as his Savior and can now give thanks even for his leprosy.

A minister to the mountain people wrote of his appreciation for the broadcasts. He had been deeply discouraged because of an illness for which he had to be hospitalized three times and had to have major surgery. He says the program was the source of his strength during the darkest moment of his life: "It helps me to overcome fear and worries during my confinement. Praise the Lord, I am now becoming stronger. My doctor informed me I could return to work next year."

PROTECTION

We had some excitement last night. At 3:15 a.m. Bonnie wakened us to tell us she heard men talking outside her window saying "Americanos!" Harold called the police and then put me on the phone while he went to investigate (armed with Steve's baseball bat). Soon the police came and followed Harold around to check the yard and roof. We have rather high walls around the homes here, but from the roof the police could see that the people who live in the place behind us were standing in their yard.

We learned that the wife had awakened in the night to see a man with a knife taking money from her husband's pants pocket. He took 40 pesos (about $6) and left. Apparently he and his partner then came over the wall into our yard but for some reason were scared off.

Praise God for His protection! Bonnie said she believed an angel must have wakened her at just the right time. The next day she "happened" to stumble across Psalm 4:8, which says, "I will both lay me down in peace and sleep: for thou, Lord only makest me dwell in safety."

13

APPROVE YOUR FISH!

"How would you like your steak?" is a pretty common question in the States (if you can afford it!). But it's quite the thing here to approve your fish before it is cooked. At a Chinese restaurant we watched the waiter net a nice big fat one, put it on a tray and bring it to a nearby table with its fins still flapping. I had shrimp.

14

AMAZING GRACE

Japanese are now visiting the Philippines in large numbers, a new phenomenon in this country which suffered so much in WWII.

One night we had dinner in the home of the Muratas, a delightful couple who are in Manila with FEBC doing Japanese programing. After dinner we chatted in their living room. Warm thoughts were going through my mind about how magnanimous it was of the Philippine people to put aside the past and accept this dear Japanese couple into their country.

Nancy was occupying herself by looking at a picture book of the history of Japan. "What's that, Mommy?" she asked in a voice clearly heard by all of us in the room. She was pointing at something in the book. With dismay I saw it was a picture of that well-known mushroom-shaped cloud of the A-bomb dropped on Japan. In silent desperation I looked to Harold to answer her question.

"Well, honey," he said quietly, "that was a bomb. . . ."

Amazing grace that enables a Japanese couple to invite an American family to dinner on Philippine soil!

LEARNING ABOUT FAMILIES

There is no divorce in the Philippines; if a man doesn't like his wife anymore, he can just leave her and find another woman to live with. He may have three women and three sets of children, and the families may or may not know about one another.

Here is how it often happens. A man living in the province, or countryside, may not be able to find enough work to support his family. So he goes to the city where he can find a good paying job. But it's lonely in the city, and so he looks for companionship. End result: a family in the province and a family in the city.

Other Asian cultures have their unique problems. We received a letter from a Christian in India whose third daughter wants to get married but the father doesn't have money for the dowry. He is still in debt for the marriage of his eldest daughter. His fellow workers are dishonest, take bribes, etc., and are better off financially than he. He wonders if God will meet his need.

When we arrived Harold began broadcasting "Guidelines for Family Living." Before he began he had doubts about producing a program that would be cross-cultural enough to meet the needs of Asian families. Surely the need for such a program is there. But can a Westerner speak to the needs of families in the East?

Then he was reminded that the Bible is truly a cross-cultural book. God doesn't have one Bible for the West and another for the East. The principles of God's Word are as valid for Asian families as for American families.

As I was leaving the market one afternoon Ginny Larson introduced herself as a missionary working in Batanes, northernmost island of the Philippines. She asked for permission to translate Guidelines' materials into the Batanes language, since there is a very real need among these people for instruction in Christian family living. Henry Ang, FEBC's broadcaster to Burma, wants to translate scripts in the Burmese language as soon as we are able to provide them for him. A lady from Southern Luzon tells us that pastors in that area are listening faithfully and some are taping the programs because of the need for counseling help. It wasn't until coming to the Philippines that we fully realized such a program was so much needed in Asia.

16

HOUSEGIRLS

The subject of househelp is a somewhat touchy one. If missionaries mention in their newsletter that they have "housegirls," all kinds of mental images come to the minds of the folks at home. Some picture a scene of posh luxury where uniformed servants cater to the slightest whim of the man and lady of the house; others imagine slave labor where the white master stands over the sweating servant with a whip. Somewhere between those two extremes lies the truth of the matter: In the tropics it is a tremendous aid to the missionary to have some help with the chores.

Househelp is probably the missionary wife's number one blessing and number one problem, and I suppose that can only be understood by experience. But I will try to explain.

In Manila the marketing alone takes one full day a week. Fruits and vegetables are bargained for at the public market. Hamburger is best bought at a frozen food store a forty-five-minute drive across the city. Canned goods and staples are cheapest at the supermarket another thirty-minute drive away. Little ready-made clothing is available, so there are numerous trips to the tailor and dressmaker for fittings.

Meals must be planned well in advance because there are almost no ready-to-eat prepared foods.

Baking is done "from scratch," and the kitchen temperature often reaches the high nineties.

Anyone who has vacationed in Florida in the summertime without the benefit of air conditioning knows how fast the laundry hamper fills up in a tropical climate.

Yes, a missionary wife can do all the work herself. But that is *all* she will do. And so she must make a decision as to what her priorities will be.

Add to this the fact that the house must never be left without someone to watch it. I must admit that I never did get used to having the girls living with us, yet I don't know what I would have done without them. But I never realized before what a part of our culture our privacy is. Nothing makes Filipinos happier than to be ever-surrounded with friends, whereas we Americans want our social life and our private life to be two separate entities. And we American women are especially used to having the kitchen as our own "turf."

Usually any problem that developed with the girls was one of communication. I'll give you some examples.

One evening we had two fine medical doctors for dinner. Our two helpers, as we call them, had done a lovely job preparing and serving dinner. Now it was time for dessert. The girls brought out bowls filled with chocolate syrup with a bit of Dream Whip topping. For the life of me, I couldn't figure out why they were serving us chocolate syrup when I had asked for chocolate sundaes. Mentally I began to review my conversation with them earlier in the day. The light began to dawn.

I remembered that after asking them to prepare chocolate sundaes, I had found some Dream Whip topping in the refrigerator. Thinking how nice that would be on the sundaes, I asked the girls to put a dab of Dream Whip on top of the chocolate syrup. Enough said?

On one occasion a missionary had a new helper who had never before made cookies. So the lady helped the girl mix the dough and then told her to shape them the size of walnuts—not realizing that walnuts do not grow in the Philippines. Results: three cookies the size of coconuts!

This same missionary was having company for dinner and had bought a large fish which she asked the girl to prepare. She explained that she would like it to be especially nice and suggested the girl tuck a little parsley behind its ear for decoration. Dinner time came and the girl served the fish—with sprigs of parsley tucked behind HER ears!

In all these instances we assumed that the girls knew something they didn't know. And we assumed we were communicating. At any rate, we had a good laugh!

The missionary must learn that it is very important to Asians that they not "lose face." Seldom will a person tell you that he does not understand what you are explaining to him. His or her answer to your question will be "yes" 90 percent of the time. A girl will do her very best to please, but she will do something the wrong way rather than ask how to do it—such an admission would cause her to lose face.

One of the greatest joys of househelp is the joy of contributing to the spiritual life of the girls. They become "members of the family" whose happiness and burdens we share. Many a helper has come to know the Lord and grown in Him as the result of living in the home of a missionary.

17

DOCTOR SALA

I would like to have been with Harold (I think) the week he spent in northern Luzon. The trip came about at the invitation of Dr. Sarmiento, a Filipino physician who also holds a theological degree and has a deep concern for both the spiritual and physical needs of the tribal people. He and his wife, a U.S.-trained cardiologist, spent a year working with the tribes.

Dr. Sarmiento, Harold, a dentist and a group of medical students flew about 275 miles north of Manila in a Philippine Air Force plane (a 1942 DC-3 well-peppered with holes, but compliments of the government, so who's to complain!) to Bagabag. There, the Summer Institute of Linguistics, better known in the U.S. as Wycliffe Bible Translators, has its base center for northern Luzon. For three days Harold had teaching sessions with the medical students and SIL staff on discipleship. He particularly challenged the med students to give a year of their practice in tribal areas. Not only would this be a great blessing to the mountain people but it would free the missionaries of medical work so that they could concentrate on translation, teaching, and evangelism.

After giving Harold a crash course in diagnosis, the group split up in teams and were flown in to the Ifugao and Ilocano areas to do medical work.

The three most common maladies of adults in this region are malaria, tuberculosis and peptic ulcers, the latter coming from chewing the narcotic betel nut.

Harold, whose doctorate is in English Bible, not medicine, would listen to their lungs with a stethoscope and if he heard gurgling sounds, he was to give them the six-month TB cure. If they complained of pain in their stomachs that went clear through to their backs, they got the ulcer medication. There was also medicine for malaria. For anything else they were sent to the third-year medical student. But he said the Filipinos seemed to prefer the American "doctor" because they had heard how good American doctors are!

About dusk the believers began to arrive for a service. In wooden houses built on stilts and illumined with oil lamps, they sang and worshipped the Lord together. A number of these people had learned to speak English, and Harold taught them choruses. His message was translated into two tribal languages.

The Ifugaos were once headhunters. Wycliffe missionaries worked for five years in this tribe with no results, and considered them nearly unreachable. But finally the language helper, Ilat, accepted Christ as Savior. He became a burning evangelist, and now there are about one hundred believers as the result of his witness. No denomination, no church building, but a vital part of the body of Christ. Before he became a Christian, Ilat was the man who sacrificed the pigs to the spirits for his people. Now he was Harold's translator. His home is about twenty-five miles away. But that is no deterrent. He walks all over the mountains sharing the gospel. Ken Kruzan, missionary pilot, says it's a joy to take Ilat in the plane with him because all the time he is flying he is watching the mountains below for people yet to be reached, noting the geography and figuring some way he can get to them to tell them about Christ.

Harold preached until his teammates fell asleep, but they were all up at four o'clock the next morning. The second night the service lasted until midnight and the people just slept on the floor.

The mountain people were very friendly and generous with what they had. A typical menu was rice for breakfast, rice for lunch, and rice for dinner, with a local vegetable and perhaps a chicken's back chopped up in it. The only time Harold had a problem eating was one breakfast when, after cutting up a chicken and putting it in a pot of water, the cook tied the entrails in a knot and threw them in, too.

Harold introduced several "significant cultural advances" to the tribal children—Tic-Tac-Toe, the game of Dots, and The Fine Art of Frisbee Throwing. But it was the men who quickly took over the Frisbee Throwing, laughing and racing through the rice paddies in their G-strings to make a retrieve.

WHY?

Each evening after Harold finished his message, the Ifugao people would ask questions. If the Christian leader could answer them, he would do so directly. If not, he would translate the question into English for Harold to answer.

There seemed to be a lot of discussion going on about one particular question. The leader stunned Harold when he finally turned to him and said, "This man wants to know: Why should I, who have so little, give to God, Who has so much?"

Harold looked around him. The people were very poorly dressed. They lived on what they could raise themselves. Money was extremely scarce. Harold wondered to himself what they really had to give. Yet, they had been learning from God's Word that they should give. What *does* God expect of these people, poor as they are?

His mind was then drawn back to the Word of God, our authority for all Christian teaching and practice. Three reasons came to his mind:

1. Because God commands it.
2. Because God has promised to bless those who give.
3. Because it is God's plan for spreading the gospel to those who have not yet heard.

If God asks poor mountain tribal people to give, how much more must He desire from us?

CHINESE DINNER

We were invited for dinner to the home of Mariano Godinez, a Manila stock broker and faithful listener to our radio program, "Guidelines."

The food was excellent. First they placed white, nearly transparent, fried noodles in our bowls and spooned soup over them. Then came roast pork with tiny whole sweet potatoes and onions, shrimp in fried *lumpia* (a rice "tortilla"), fried rice, and a mixed vegetable dish of peas, carrots, whole mushrooms, miniature whole ears of corn, and hardboiled quail eggs, which are the size of bird eggs and delicious! Dessert was shredded young coconut in coconut milk, slices of mango and watermelon.

When Mr. Godinez had invited us, he mentioned he was having several friends in after dinner. As it turned out, Harold gave an extemporaneous Bible study to about thirty people.

Mrs. Godinez told us, "Before World War Two I didn't care much about going to church. But when the war broke out and I could not attend, I really felt the loss. And ever since, I don't want to miss if only to show gratitude to the Lord for the freedom of believers to meet together."

20

BALUT: FILIPINO DELICACY

Here's a Filipino delicacy you wouldn't get in the United States: balut (pronounced bah-LOOT). I quote from our Manila newspaper:

> Balut, as most Filipinos know, is the eighteen-day-old fertilized duck egg, hard-boiled, and relished by gourmets. Balut-eating involves a gastronomic ritual that has to be followed strictly if one is to enjoy the delicacy. First, the gourmet must puncture a hole on the rotund end of the egg, suck the liquid out. Then he must widen the hole, sprinkle on some salt to taste and pick out the chick in two or three bits. First-timers are advised to eat their balut with eyes closed.

A balut vendor goes by our house each evening. The children once bought one out of curiosity and dissected it. But when my father came to visit, he did what few American tourists accomplish—he ate an entire balut. Yuk!

21

PNEUMONIA

Harold had the flu, got up too soon, had a relapse, and now Dr. Sarmiento says he has bronchial pneumonia. But the fever is gone and with antibiotics and a series of vitamin shots and rest he'll be okay.

The front page of the paper today said, "Skin-deep winter has come to the Philippines with the advent of chilly mornings." The article went on to say that the winds are now blowing down from Siberia and the cold weather has set in. Lest you envision us buried in snow, let me explain that this is the first time this year the temperature in Manila has dropped below seventy degrees. I just *had* to tease Harold about getting pneumonia the week the weather turned "cold!"

When he got an X-ray at the hospital, Harold noticed several copies of his booklet "Guidelines for Peace of Mind" in the cashier's window. He learned that Dr. Sarmiento had distributed them in the hospital. One day an obstetrician saw a nurse with one and asked to borrow it while waiting for a baby to arrive. It was the tool God used to bring the doctor to accept Christ as Savior. Also this booklet was used to lead one of Dr. Sarmiento's patients to the Lord. Her gifts made possible the building of a clinic among the tribal people.

22

CHRISTMAS

We have decorated our palm plant for Christmas, lights and all. Paper lanterns, with or without lights, are the big Christmas decoration in the Philippines, some very elaborate, all very colorful, all handmade and inexpensive. The kids are elated to find that fireworks are legal here this time of year. There go their allowances up in smoke!

On Christmas Sunday morning Harold preached in a Filipino church. The Sunday school play was especially realistic to me because everyone, of course, had brown faces. The ever-faithful bathrobes (how could we ever have Christmas plays without them!) served well as costumes. The Air Force general with whom we had dinner a few weeks earlier wore one to play Herod, ad-libbing as he came on stage: "That tailor does a terrible job of fitting my clothes. This robe—why, just look at it. It fits like a bathrobe!"

I find it more enjoyable to make this a Filipino Christmas than merely to try to duplicate the way we do things in the States. At first the kids were pessimistic about being in a foreign country for Christmas. But that changed. Bonnie summed it up: "Christmas is going to be nice. Some things are really different, but the main part—about Jesus—is the same!"

I must admit at first I was tempted to shield my-

41

self against homesickness by inwardly glossing over Christmas. But this would be like shutting Christ out, for it is His birthday. So, full steam ahead! After all, *He* was born in a "foreign country."

ON THE ROAD TO BAGUIO

We left at sunrise for Luzon's mile-high resort town of Baguio. I wish I had a photographic memory to capture all the scenes along the way. To western eyes, unaccustomed to nipa huts, carabao, rice terraces, and banana trees, traveling in the provinces is like walking through the pages of *National Geographic*. Sometimes we stop and take pictures, but on a two-lane road jammed with buses, trucks, oxcarts, jeepneys, tricycles, children, and animals, one doesn't stop unnecessarily. Besides, in several areas where they are repairing the shoulder of the road there is an eighteen-inch drop-off.

I'm too new in this country not to be stirred by what I see here. Puffy clouds and blue sky reflected in the mirror-waters of the rice paddies. A silver-haired woman smoking her thin cigar. Families living in hovels made of assorted scrap metal while others live in homes ornate with wrought iron. Vivid *bougainvillea* and poinsettias by the roadsides. The most brilliant green of young rice fields. In a sari-sari store, a picture of the thorn-crowned Christ propped up on a shelf of Pepsis. A man dressed in a G-string—*and* a long-sleeved sweatshirt. A goat riding on the roof of a bus along with the baggage. Shy children with runny eyes. Men carrying heavy sacks of rice on their backs while women carry vegetables on their heads.

The beauty we would like to photograph. The poverty—no.

24

FAITH ACADEMY

Probably the greatest influence on our children during these two years is Faith Academy. Here about five hundred MKs (missionary kids) from kindergarten through high school receive quality education in a sound Christian atmosphere. The entire faculty receive no pay but raise their support as missionaries themselves before coming overseas. We missionaries owe them a debt of gratitude. Without them we could not do what we're doing.

An experience I will not forget is attending Faith Academy Association meetings. I wish I could describe the thrill of being in a room packed with several hundred missionaries engaged in such a vast gamut of Christian ministries: literature, seminary teaching, church planting, outreach to China, evangelism, Christian education, medical work, radio, helping the poor, Bible translation. . . . "Electric" is the word that describes the feeling there. It was a foretaste of that day when we will *all* be gathered together to sing God's praises for eternity.

One meeting featured a quick pictorial history of the school. After seeing how it started in the city twenty years ago with a rickety old house, two teachers, and practically no money, I think they named the school correctly. Now the simple but neat buildings are located on a knoll outside Manila in what has become a country club area. And the cool breeze is something the city-folks envy.

ANIMAL LIFE

Coming back from Faith Academy I had to stop the car to let a lizard cross the road—not the kind we have in our house but a three-foot-long one. He took his time getting across while I told myself, "This is for real—I'm not at the zoo." When he reached the other side, he disappeared into the tall grass, and we watched it sway as he made his way through.

When I told Harold about this, he said, "Do you remember that only a few weeks ago they killed a nine-foot python on the sidewalk in front of FEBC's administration building?" It seems the Far East Broadcasting Company's compound was a Japanese snake farm during the war and there are still a few "descendants" there.

A NEEDY WORLD

Such a vast gamut of needs in the lives of those who write in response to the broadcasts! In answering some of the letters in just one day we promised to pray for:

1. A fourteen-year-old girl who is rebelling against her parents and asks for help.

2. A Filipino medical student who asks advice about leaving his studies for the ministry.

3. A young single girl in India (Bible woman) who must counsel those much older than herself and is hesitant to give advice.

4. A man who says he is a loner and hints at suicide.

5. A woman nearly overcome by fear.

6. A young man with a personal sin so big he wonders if God can forgive.

7. Support missionaries in the "boonies" of Colombia who are thankful for the program.

"A" CERTIFICATES

Monday

We spent the entire morning getting our "A" certificates of registration today. We were told to go to City Hall. First stop, eleventh floor: wrong office. Second stop, fourteenth floor: wrong office, wrong building. Down to ground floor, over two buildings and up to second floor: wrong office, still wrong building. Down to ground floor and to another building where after waiting in line for about half an hour we were finally successful in getting what we needed.

Tuesday

Today I saw a sign which says we could have gotten our "A" certificates right on the compound where we live! Things you learn your first year in a foreign country!

JESUS IS LORD!

One morning our helper Pat, who is a Christian, asked if she could talk to us for a few minutes. Sitting down in the office, she began to tell us something that came as quite a shock. Our second helper, Marilyn, was having a visitor during the night, she said. "He is courting Marilyn," she continued, "and wants her to marry him."

The two girls share a bedroom just off the kitchen in the back half of the house. Harold has installed special locks on all the outside doors which he checks himself each night—first of all for our personal safety, and second because we have several thousand dollars' worth of equipment in the office and recording studio. One of the reasons we have the girls living with us is that it is unwise ever to leave a home unattended here. The idea that someone was coming in during the night without our being aware of it was disconcerting, to say the least.

At first I thought perhaps she was having nightmares. After questioning Pat very carefully, however, we began to recognize that Marilyn's visitor was no bad dream but was actually an evil spirit. The events of the days that followed removed any doubt.

That evening after dinner we invited the girls to join us for a Bible study on what the devil is like.

Harold underlined verses about resisting Satan in Marilyn's Bible such as I Peter 5:8, 9, James 4:7, II Corinthians 4:4, and John 8:44. After carefully explaining how to become a Christian, Harold asked Marilyn if she would like to accept Christ as her Savior now. She said, "Yes."

"All right, Marilyn," Harold said, "I'll pray the words and you repeat them after me."

He began, "Heavenly Father, I am a sinner and need your help. I believe Jesus died for my sin. Right now I want you to forgive me of my sin and come into my heart. I believe You will make me a new person as You promised. Thank you for saving me right now. In Jesus' name, Amen."

Being very shy in nature and hesitant to speak up, Marilyn would not pray out loud, so Harold asked, "Marilyn, did you say those words in your heart as I prayed?" She nodded, "Yes."

Two days later, about ten o'clock in the evening, Marilyn's visitor came again—this time tormenting her rather than courting her. Missionaries who were guests in our home that evening joined us in special prayer. Marilyn developed a sudden fever of 104°. When I gave her medicine, she refused to take it and instead flung it across the room, entirely contrary to her quiet, agreeable nature. She would lie on her bed and moan and groan, then get up and pace through the house as if in pain. Some rooms she would not enter because, she said, there were "people" in them. She refused to sit on the sofa because "men" were there. Harold prayed earnestly for her and rebuked Satan. But when he did, Marilyn said the "man" laughed, and Harold looked to her to be the ugliest person she had ever seen. We prayed with her until midnight, and several Christian girls continued until nearly four in the morning. Marilyn said the "visitor" told her he would be back the next evening at ten o'clock for her answer.

Sure enough, the next evening at ten o'clock this began all over again following the weekly girls' Bible study held in our home. Marilyn was again tormented. At times she could not see, and she spoke very little. She would wander through the house as if searching for something. Picking up Harold's Bible, she began to flip frantically through the pages. Then she flung it down. (Later she told us she was looking for the verses Harold had read to her, but the pages were all blank.) We were beginning to get desperate.

The climax came that evening when Harold took Marilyn into the living room and insisted she sit down. He began to urge her to repeat after him, "Jesus is my Savior, Jesus is my Lord! Satan, leave me alone!" But she would not. (Later she told us she could not because the demon would clap his hand over her mouth.) Harold instructed her that she must exercise her will against the demon and rebuke the devil herself. She seemed to want to but couldn't.

Harold says that suddenly he knew exactly how Paul felt in Acts 16:18 when he was greatly annoyed in his spirit with the devil. "Marilyn," Harold asked, "Do you want me to command this spirit to leave you?" A frightened girl nodded affirmatively.

Turning to her directly, he commanded the deaf and dumb demon to leave her, in the name of Jesus. In one last display of anger the demon struck her, Marilyn said, and was gone. Her speech returned. Tears filling her eyes, she could now say, "Jesus is my Lord! Thank you, Jesus!"

"He's gone, Marilyn," said Harold. "It's all over. Go in and tell the others what God has done."

A dozen girls who had been praying were now hugging one another and crying with joy. We had another time of prayer that night—this time praise to God for His power which is greater than any we may come up against. Praise Him! Truly, He is Lord!

GOOD LISTENERS

This afternoon I spoke to a group of Chinese high school and college young people at Youth Gospel Center in the heart of Manila. The songs were in English, but before making the announcements in Chinese, the leader apologized to me—so polite!

Most of the Chinese now living in the Philippines were born here of families which emigrated years ago from the mainland of China. They are usually involved in the business life of the Philippines.

Speaking to an Asian audience is a bit different than speaking to an American audience. There isn't much change of facial expression, so it's hard for the speaker to judge whether or not he is getting his message across. But the rewarding part is that people here are excellent listeners and remember much of what they hear. Also, they are not supersaturated with Christian messages from radio, TV, and special meetings as we are in most parts of the States. We found the people to be warm, receptive, and very appreciative.

30

ANTS IN THE SUGAR

I understand you can tell how long a missionary has been in the Philippines by how she reacts to the ants in the sugar:

Year one: She finds ants in the sugar; she throws the sugar out.

Year two: She finds ants in the sugar; she picks out every one.

Year three: She finds ants in the sugar; she picks out most of them.

Year four: She finds sugar *without* ants and asks, "Where's the protein?"

A missionary I met recently has been living the last few months in a small *barrio* while learning the local dialect. One day she was ready to frost a cake and found that her only box of confectioners' sugar was full of ants. So . . . she made *chocolate* frosting! She is more "adjusted" than I am!

LETTERS FROM EDWARD

Edward wrote several years ago in response to a Guidelines program about the five missionaries who were killed by the Aucas in Ecuador. In that letter he challenged, "What did their faith do for them? All they got was a spear in the belly!"

In answering his letter Harold pointed out Edward's need for the Lord. But Edward thought he didn't need anyone.

Years passed and we forgot about Edward's letter until he wrote again. After losing family, job and home and even getting into Satan worship, at the end of himself, he was approached by a girl from Avalon Jesus Center in Akron, Ohio. Edward gave his life to Jesus and now writes to tell us of the miracles that have taken place in his life. He has gotten his job back and has lost his craving for liquor. Even as those missionaries to the Aucas in Ecuador, he has committed his life to Someone worth dying for. A satanist high priest put a curse on him when he learned he was saved, but Edward is claiming "Greater is He that is in you than he that is in the world." Now he waits to hear Guidelines each day.

"CHRIST DIED FOR OUR SINS . . ."

Easter vacation! Back to Baguio again.

On the way, we passed through Pampanga, where on Good Friday several men would allow themselves to be actually crucified for ten to twenty minutes. We saw a man dressed in a robe dragging his cross along the highway. Another was lying on the ground with a large cross on top of him.

On Friday some known as *flagellantes* will whip themselves with thongs, then wash their bloody backs in the river in hopes of atoning for their sins and the sins of loved ones. It is sad they do not realize:

> There is a fountain filled with blood drawn from
> Immanuel's veins,
> And sinners plunged beneath that flood lose all
> their guilty stains.

EASTER

The day began with a sunrise service at 5:30 a.m. in a little concrete-block Filipino church. The building is not completed yet. For people who earn $1.25 a day, church-building is a slow process. But it is a growing church with many young people.

After this early service, Easter breakfast was served at the church: rolls, hard-boiled eggs, potato salad, and hot dogs. Harold preached again at the 10 a.m. service. Then about twenty young people were baptized.

Surprisingly, Easter is not a big celebration at all in the Philippines. Good Friday is the big day with stores closed, and many radio stations playing only mournful music. On Easter it's business as usual.

As I looked across the mountaintops, a prayer rose in my heart that the light of Easter may dawn in the hearts of many more of these mountain people.

SO WHAT?

After church one Sunday evening we ate soup at a lovely carpeted Chinese restaurant with chandeliers—one of our favorites. Hardly had we started eating when Harold put his hand on mine and said, "Honey, look over there—there's a big rat under that table."

We told the waiter, but the only response we got from him was a nod. Thinking he didn't understand, Harold explained again. Very casually the waiter pointed to the wall with his pencil. "There's a hole over there, and when it rains, they come in," he said without looking up from his work. What struck me was not that there was a rat in the restaurant—understandable in a tropical climate—but the waiter's total lack of concern. "A rat? So what?"

UPHEAVAL

We talked to Bob McKee, who has just arrived from Saigon after engineering the exit of eighty-one Wycliffe missionaries from Vietnam. He put some of their people aboard the orphan flights but for some reason failed to learn of one particular flight in time to get anyone on board. It was the C-5 Galaxy that crashed outside Saigon, killing two hundred.

Many missionaries had to leave behind everything they owned. The parents of a student at Faith Academy were allowed to leave Vietnam with only their Bible translation and two changes of clothing. Their house was burned.

Last night a girl who has just arrived from Cambodia urged us to pray for the thousands who turned to Christ there in the last months before the Red Khmer takeover. Desperate, they saw no hope but Christ. Now we must pray they will stand under persecution.

GOD'S TIMETABLE

April 10, 1975:

Nothing short of a direct act of God brought Bich Hoang to Manila today from Saigon. Bich is the FEBC broadcaster who does the translation of Guidelines into the Vietnamese language. The miracle is that South Vietnam granted her, a full-blooded Vietnamese, clearance to leave—when even Vietnamese wives of Americans cannot yet get out. She brought her daughter with her, but her husband, a South Vietnamese army chaplain, had to stay behind. So did the other Vietnamese broadcasters and their children. Only the Lord knows what their fate will be. Being Christians and also in the media, they are third in priority on the lists for liquidation when Saigon falls to the Vietcong. It appears that will happen in a matter of days now.

April 20

We learned that the Vietnamese broadcasters had an opportunity to leave Vietnam by boat but turned it down because they did not feel this was God's way out. How thankful they were that they had been sensitive to the Spirit's direction—they later learned that the boat was discovered, its passengers arrested and jailed.

April 23

At 1:30 this morning FEBC received a phone call saying all the Vietnamese staff and their families have been flown to the Philippines and are now at Clark Air Force Base. Praise God!

How precise is God's timing in bringing these people here just as FEBC's new 250,000-watt radio station goes on the air. This station will blanket Southeast Asia and much of China with a signal that can be picked up on a simple transistor radio. Missionaries cannot go there now, but radio can. And the staff will be available for programming.

AIRLIFT TO FREEDOM

Harold spoke tonight at the Christian Servicemen's Center at Clark Air Force Base and we presented a musical package. Many of the Christian women are deeply involved in caring for the orphans as they arrive at the Base from Vietnam and Cambodia. They are darling children. They have been uprooted from their homeland, but are given the blessing of freedom. Some are ill from the change in food. Some are so frightened that instead of eating their food they hide it in their clothing for fear that they won't have something to eat the next time they are hungry. One baby weighed less than two pounds. Another was only three days old. Many arrived with sores and diseases, yet only a very few out of many hundreds have died. The Base gymnasium houses them, and each one is assigned a volunteer mother for a six-hour shift. Some of the "mothers" are teenage boys—they are doing a great job.

DAY OF CONTRASTS

The church Harold preached in this morning has thirty outstations, and ministers primarily to a re-settlement area whose people have been relocated from Manila slums to an area outside the city. They speak Ilocano, one of the many dialects of the Philippines, so Harold's message had to be interpreted.

The church building is open on the sides, and a delightful breeze swept through. Two friendly hound dogs wandered in and out, much to the entertainment of our children. When it came time for the sermon the dogs comfortably sprawled out in the aisle and went to sleep. There was a good response to the invitation. After the service we were all served bright purple, yellow, and white rice cakes in banana leaves.

Just one hour later we were on the fourteenth floor of the Intercontinental Hotel for a marvelous buffet dinner. Intricate butter carvings and a four-foot high ice mold decorated the table.

Sometimes my mind has a hard time catching up with my body here. The contrasts are so great!

As guests of two Filipino Christian doctors, we had an outstanding meal. But the best part of the dinner was sharing the company of Dr. Raymond Benson, a surgeon who had been serving with Medical Ambassadors in Dalat in the Central Highlands of Vietnam. He and his wife had to leave a week ago, as did many hundreds of other missionaries, with only a suitcase. Hardest of all was leaving behind 150,000 Highland Christians, whose future is uncertain.

THE ONLY ANSWER

Psychological warfare was a prime tool of the Vietcong, reported Dr. Benson. Such tactics are far worse, he said, than conventional warfare because in psychological warfare everyone loses.

A couple of weeks before, Dr. Benson went down to the village marketplace, colorful with fruits and vegetables and brightly dressed peasants. He stopped at the bank to visit with its president, a good friend.

As they chatted they heard a commotion. Stepping out on the veranda overlooking the marketplace, they saw people frantically running in every direction. It was complete panic.

They stopped someone long enough to ask what had happened. "The Vietcong are in the marketplace!" they were told. Within minutes the marketplace was emptied of absolutely everything—fruits, vegetables and people.

Dr. Benson said he walked out of the bank and across the silent marketplace. Not a single Vietcong soldier was there. He had witnessed panic based on pure fear.

Then Dr. Benson explained. For the past twenty years the Vietcong had been unexpectedly sweeping into little villages of no military value and machine-gunning women and children. Then they would take the head man of the village, often the

66

pastor, to the center of the town and publicly torture him—perhaps cut out his tongue, gouge out his eyes, or bury him up to his neck and leave him there to die. Is it any wonder that the Vietcong could sometimes take a village with no opposition?

But, said Dr. Benson, the answer to absolute fear is absolute faith. And then he told us of Jimmy, his Vietnamese fellow-worker. Jimmy would accompany him on his travels through the Highlands and interpret for him when he preached. Though he was a very small man, Jimmy preached with tremendous anointing from the Lord, and many hundreds turned to Christ.

When it came time for Dr. Benson to say goodbye to Jimmy at the airport, his eyes filled with tears. "Jimmy, don't you want to come with me on the plane? Perhaps I could get clearance for you."

"No, no," said Jimmy, "I will stay here."

"But Jimmy, where will you go? There is no place for you to go."

"I will go back to my people in the Highlands and tell them about Christ."

"But Jimmy, you're sure to suffer at the hands of the Vietcong. They may torture you and kill you."

Dr. Benson said Jimmy's face lighted up. "That doesn't matter, sir, for then I will be with Jesus."

The only answer to absolute fear, as Dr. Benson said, is absolute faith in Jesus Christ.

40

MY TURN IN BAGABAG

My daughter Nancy and I flew to Bagabag for a two-week visit at Wycliffe's base for northern Luzon. Is it ever hot! I tried to take a nap the first afternoon but the little red ants invaded. At night Nancy had a hard time going to sleep for fear a flying roach would land on her.

Each evening we have dinner with a different family. I feel I'm learning a lot just listening.

The Center, located several miles from town, is flat, grassy and dotted with about a dozen nice homes plus the study center and a plane hangar. Three pilots and their families live here permanently along with the base supervisor. The rest of the homes are occupied by translators who live for two to three months among the people who speak the dialect they are studying. They then return to the base to develop what they have learned, and go back to the tribe for another two or three months. This Center services about fifteen teams.

The generator is turned off at 9:30, but we're quite ready to sleep by then.

FROM ISOLATION TO CIVILIZATION

Francis, an Ifugao language helper, returned to Bagabag today after a year in the U.S. and Canada helping a missionary finish a translation. He told us that his first night in the States he could not sleep a wink because there was a bird in the house which sang every hour. The next morning he learned about cuckoo clocks.

For his first public service, he told us he put on his headdress, G-string, scabbard and spear. But some people laughed and others looked scared; so he didn't try that again. Imagine all the experiences he has to share with his wife and family!

42

"GO YE THEREFORE, AND TEACH ALL NATIONS"

Jan Headland, a translator, showed me pictures of the Dumagots, the tribe she and her husband Tom are working with. These people are negritos, possibly the original Filipinos, but they rank very low on the social scale. She also showed me a picture of the six-hundred-pound snake shot by one of their men: a python twenty-six inches in circumference and nearly twenty-three feet long. It was too large and tough to be good eating, she said.

In the pictures Jan pointed out a number of people who accepted Christ and four couples who have been baptized. Some of these Christians are already now with the Lord.

The Headlands have translated every book in the New Testament except for four, and I am to do some typing to help on those. Because the New People's Army (Communists) have been very active in their area, they must determine whether it is safe to return.

43

MOUNTAIN PEOPLE

I have now finished typing what is called a "back translation" of the Book of Philippians—a translation of the dialect version of Scripture back into English. It is a paraphrase that fits beautifully the culture of the tribe and the idioms of its language. Regardless of our language and culture, human nature is the same, and I enjoyed the word pictures the translator used.

A special treat came when JARS* pilot Ken Kruzan said there was room for me on a flight into the mountains. First stop was Bunhiin, where Dr. Sarmiento is supervising the building of a clinic. Then we flew on to Natunin, where Ken was to pick up a missionary and a lady who needed hospitalization. When we landed there were two sick people and their companions. So Ken asked if I would stay behind, and he would come back for me.

I had a delightful hour in Natunin. Steep mountains, brilliant green rice terraces, and beautiful valleys surrounded me. (The famed Banaue rice terraces are not far from this spot.) I found a believer who knew English. There are about fifty believers in this place, she said.

The people who met the plane invited me into their little house on stilts. So after climbing the

*Jungle Aviation and Radio Service (JARS) is an arm of Wycliffe Bible Translators.

little ladder, I sat on a tiny stool about the height of a brick and had a fine chat with two elderly ladies and my "interpreter." The house had two small rooms. Bundles of unhusked rice were stacked in one corner (they pound it fresh every day) and the fireplace with its blackened ricepots was on the floor in another corner. The women, tattooed all over their arms and shoulders, were chewing betel nut and lime, which gives them bright red mouths and lips. I've never met friendlier people.

The wind was picking up, and it crossed my mind that the plane might not be able to get back in. (As hospitable as the people were, I'm sure they would have taken me in.) But Ken did make it, and we bounced on back to the Center.

By the way, these are the people for whom I just typed Philippians.

44

A JOY NOT DEPENDENT ON CIRCUMSTANCES

After the electricity went off, I lay in bed listening to what sounded to me like two mice playing tag in the bathroom. Carrying in the kerosene lamp, I saw not mice but two huge cockroaches. Repelled by the light, the two noisemakers squeezed out through the unlocked screen door and—you can laugh if you like, but I declare it's true—the door shut after they went through!

After spraying the window frame and the legs of my bed, I'm at least free of ants in bed now. Maybe they should call this place *Bugabug* instead of Bagabag.

Yet I love it here. It's my observation that the other missionaries love it too. I've learned firsthand that when God sends you to a place, He gives joy and contentment—never mind the bugs!

HOW DO YOU WRITE AN OBITUARY?

A very wealthy Christian lady in Manila called for help in writing her grandfather's obituary. She wanted something different from the usual "Pray for the repose of his soul" that is used in this country. Harold was away, so I added one more unique experience to the list of Things I Never Thought I'd Do as a Missionary—write a millionaire's obituary!

"EVERY ONE THAT HATH FORSAKEN CHILDREN FOR MY NAME'S SAKE. . . ."

Angie wore her best long dress to church that Sunday morning in Manila, for there was to be a wedding—her son's wedding. And she was excited.

But as I watched her, a lump rose in my throat. Angie is an FEBC missionary; her husband is a brilliant engineer who builds radio stations. (Their salary is a fraction of what it would be in commercial radio.) And their son Mark was being married on Saturday evening in the U.S., at the same time Angie was attending church Sunday morning halfway around the world in Manila. I knew Angie and her husband hadn't had the money to make the trip for the wedding.

When I asked her how she could make such a sacrifice, she brushed it off with a comment about the fact that Mark had come to visit them in Manila a few months before. She wasn't complaining.

I still had a lump in my throat.

FACES

Harold preached at the United Evangelical Church this morning, Manila's largest Chinese congregation. The children and I came rather early and were seated at the front. When the pastor introduced our family (in Chinese—I was hoping I'd know when to stand!), it was quite an experience to turn around and look into seven or eight hundred Chinese faces, each framed with black hair.

I got to thinking: for every person in that congregation there are more than a million people in mainland China who cannot meet together as we did for Christian worship.

CHINA BORDER

Hong Kong is an exciting city, and it's especially beautiful at night.

We're the guests of Buddy and Martie Gaines, missionaries with OMS International.* Today they drove us through the New Territories, past walled cities several hundreds of years old. We stopped at one of these cities to visit an evangelical church and to meet the pastor.

Ten minutes later we were at the China border looking across a broad green valley. Down through the valley flows a river, the division between communism and freedom. Across the river I could see a small village such as we had visited ten minutes before. Yet I know there is no evangelical church building there.

As we drove away from the border, I commented to Martie, "The best part is that we can drive back home on *this* side of the river."

Wisely she corrected me, "It would be better if we could drive across to the *other* side of the river."

*Formerly The Oriental Missionary Society, Inc.

LECHON

Friends of Fred Magbanua, director of FEBC Philippines, honored his birthday tonight with a dinner featuring *lechon*—roasted suckling pig. The pig was delivered whole, already cooked, wrapped in foil, and accompanied by two carvers. Their first job was to cut off the head and place it on the table as a centerpiece. The meat was delicious. In fact, the whole meal was. My favorites were *lumpia*, similar to Chinese egg roll, and a meat dish made primarily of chopped banana blossom.

On another occasion when we were invited to a *lechon* dinner we were also served a cup of dark liquid which looked like soup or broth. Upon asking, we learned it was pig's blood.

"No, thank you, we just don't care for any. Please let someone else enjoy ours."

50

"THEY THAT GO DOWN
TO THE SEA. . . ."

We went to Matabuncay Beach for some snorkeling in the warm clear South China Sea—my first time, actually. Warning: here's where I get ecstatic! It's like entering another world. How can I describe the thrill when a whole school of brilliant yellow fish swims lazily by so near you could touch them, thin and round like saucers standing on their edges. Great canyons of coral in a rainbow of shades—yellow, brown, red, blue, pink, and green—make a garden setting for the fish. Sea urchins appear to be blossoms planted in nooks and crannies of the coral. (However, "Don't pick the flowers!") It's quite an experience underwater when you see the edge of the reef suddenly drop off and you feel as if you'll fall off too. Then you realize you're in a different world where you can float over drop-offs and not fall. It's like being able to fly.

What impressed me most was the lavish way God created all this beauty—way down there where relatively few people see it. When I make something I think is beautiful, I want to put it where people can see it. But God seems to have created beauty just because it is His nature to do so. He wasn't satisfied to create only gray fish. No, there is every shade imaginable in what seems to be an unending assortment of designs and color combinations—even plaids! I can't help thinking He must have a sense of humor, too, to have thought up some funny looking creatures—like the one that looked to be a walking piece of coral until I saw a mouth and eye on its bumpy, lumpy head.

"They that go down to the sea . . . these see the works of the Lord, and his wonders in the deep" (Ps. 107:23, 24).

"GOOD MORNING, VISITOR"

This morning I accompanied Harold when he spoke to 1400 high schoolers at Hope Christian School. This is a Chinese Christian day school in the heart of Manila which enrolls students from preschool age through high school. Their school day goes from 7:15 to 5:30 with instruction in Amoy, Mandarin, Tagalog, and English.

After the chapel service the principal took us on a tour of the school which included every one of the preschool and kindergarten classrooms. "Good morning, Visitor," we heard from 569 little uniformed cuties who rose and bowed. Then they were seated—quietly! Two at a desk, about forty per teacher. What discipline!

WOMEN'S RIGHTS?

The mother of twelve children asks for counsel. Her husband has just walked out on her for another woman, and she is left with twelve mouths to feed. She has no recourse except legal separation. But even that would not provide child support. Not only will the mother have to try to find work but so will the children.

Women's rights don't go very far in the Philippines. If a single woman owns property, when she marries she gives up all right to sell that property without her husband's approval. Good incentive for Filipino men to marry rich girls!

I put up a rack of free Guidelines' booklets in our local beauty shop. The books disappear quickly, partly because reading materials are expensive here compared with the daily wage. It really isn't surprising, however, that the most popular one is "Answers to Suffering," for I feel that women get the short end of life here.

TYPOGRAPHICAL ERRORS

We've just discovered a bad typographical error on one of our new Guidelines booklets: "It's futile and unnecessary to play with children." Ten thousand copies!

Our Christian editor-friend showed us a Tagalog songbook that has recently been printed here that is supposed to read "All the Way My Savior Leads." But the Chinese typesetter couldn't quite make out the handwriting, and they ended up with "All the Way My Swim Leaks."

LEARNING BY LISTENING

I wish folks at home could listen in on sharing times like we had during the service this morning at FEBC. A Filipino minister's wife told that they had been granted a scholarship and a sponsorship to go to the U.S. but could get no visa. Rather than dwell on disappointment, they have accepted this as indication that God has work for them to do in their own country. They are learning, she said, to judge circumstances by God's love rather than God's love by circumstances.

Byrd Brunemeir, an engineer who is building the radio relay system between all the FEBC stations in the Philippines, said he found it hard to reconcile Colossians 3:2 ("Set your affections on things above, not on things on the earth") with his job for several months of scouting through dirty back alleys of Manila where used electronics parts can be bought cheap. He figures he can save 90 percent of the cost of materials this way, but it's very "down-to-earth" work, not nearly as spiritually rewarding as broadcasting. Then he read on to verse 17: "And whatsoever ye do in word (broadcasting) or deed (looking for parts in grubby shops), do all in the name of the Lord Jesus. . . ."

The last person to speak was a broadcaster from Vietnam who thanked the Lord that it looks as though she will be granted a visa to stay in the

Philippines. She testified to experiencing the peace of God when last Friday she received back her own letter she had written to her mother in Saigon four days before the city fell. Not knowing if her mother is dead or alive, she said it was as if the Lord spoke to her saying, "My child, be strong, be strong in My grace."

CARABAO WALLOW

The carabao, or water buffalo, is the beast of burden of the Philippines and well suited to plowing the rice fields of the tropics.

The children's school bus route goes by the University of the Philippines Golf Course. Steve says every now and then he sees a carabao using a water hazard for his wallow. All that can be seen above the waterline are his horns and nose.

MORNING, NOON, AND NIGHT

Today has been very full. The morning began with our neighborhood missionary wives' Bible study, a great time for us to share together our problems and victories. In the afternoon I sat on a panel at the Asian Theological Seminary women's fellowship discussing how to raise "preacher's kids" and "missionary kids." Then tonight Harold spoke to the Faith Academy Association (Faith Academy's PTA) on "Why Kids Accept or Reject Their Parents' Values."

We have been greatly blessed by the fellowship of other missionaries. Somehow, the competitiveness that regretfully sometimes exists among Christian workers in the States is not strong here. Could the reason be that each missionary is so busy fighting Satan that he has little time or energy to fight his fellow missionary? I sense a strong realization that we need one another.

DOOR-TO-DOOR SALESMAN

Steve says that while we were gone a fellow came to the door selling carabao milk. "Try it," he said, "You can taste the difference!"

I bet you *can*!

ANOTHER MISSIONARY SHARES

In our missionary wives' Bible study of Psalm 40 Carol Fuller, Wycliffe missionary to Vietnam, was glad she was asked to comment on verse 5: "Many, O Lord my God, are thy wonderful works which thou has done . . . they are more than can be numbered."

Surely the events of her life bear testimony to the truth of that verse—instant healing as a child from a hemophilia-type condition that nearly took her life during a tonsillectomy; God's peace as they huddled under the stairs of their house in Saigon, one and a half blocks from the Palace, the object of intense bombing; God's protection in a Vietnamese village near their tribal area as she lay awake at night listening to machine-gun fire. Though all around them the ammunition found its mark, their place was absolutely untouched.

Then one night the tribal people insisted that for their safety they must leave immediately and not wait until morning as they had planned. Afterwards they learned morning would have been too late. Almost nine months pregnant, Carol sat on pillows in the jeep that took them down the mountains to the coast. Arriving in Manila she learned she would need a Caesarean section—not possible where they had been living in Vietnam.

The perfection of God's timing!

THANK YOU!

About fifty people found the Lord during the eleven days Harold has been in Taipei and Okinawa. He spoke in schools, military chapels, to radio personnel, at banquets and in churches.

At a dinner for radio station JOFF a Buddhist lady gave Harold two lovely Japanese dolls as an expression of thanks for Guidelines. She likes the music on JOFF but says Guidelines is the only Christian message she listens to. Then, with tears in her eyes, she added, "You know, sometimes I wonder if I'm right."

MKs

Usually Harold is the "mouthpiece" of our family—he is the one who conducts the seminars. But today I had the privilege of conducting a two-hour seminar for missionary wives on "How to Raise Well-Adjusted Missionary Kids." What a topic! I wish I had all the answers! My heart is burdened to pray more for the children of missionaries now that I've experienced some of their problems.

MILK OF THE WORD

I have begun a weekly Bible study for housegirls in our area. Many times these girls do not get the opportunity to attend church because their "Moms" want them at the house on Sundays. So they miss out on fellowship and the food of God's Word. Their English is limited, but we work hard to understand each other.

It is exciting to teach these girls because God's Word is new to most of them. While some have been Christians for a number of years, others have never read a Bible before or even known there is an Old Testament and a New Testament.

How can so much have been packed into these two years! Gratitude wells up in my heart! We have had opportunity to minister in Bible schools and seminaries, in schools for MKs; at youth camps and women's retreats; through live radio broadcasts and to radio station personnel; at breakfasts, banquets and Bible studies; at high school and college commencement exercises; at annual mission conferences—all in addition to counseling and correspondence. Not counting, of course, writing and recording twenty-five pages of radio script every week for the two Guidelines programs.

What can we say except "Great is Thy faithfulness!" Our cup runs over!

DIFFERENCES

We've been here long enough now that I don't
"see" things that I used to notice. Now and then I
remember that in the States rural people don't
shampoo their hair by the side of the road and pour
buckets of water over their heads to rinse the soap
out. Or pound their clothes with a wooden paddle.

Communication is different too. No need to call
loudly for someone—a soft "ssst" sound, and anyone nearby will turn around to see what you want.
Here a silent, quick raise of the eyebrows means
"yes." And you can give directions by just "pointing" with your lips.

In a restaurant the waiter would be embarrassed
to bring you the check before you asked for it. That
would be considered rude—like asking for money.

These things are such a part of life here that I'm
less and less aware of them.

PERSPECTIVE

I have not mentioned many of the similarities here to life in the U.S. In Manila, for instance, are some of the most beautiful homes I have ever seen. There are shopping centers like those in the United States. Education has a high priority, with 35,000 students living in the university section of the city. The Philippines is probably the most americanized country in Asia.

Yet, whatever the similarities, the needs of people cry out. Once a month we take the rent check to our landlady. On her side of the street are the high-walled homes of the wealthy. Across the street squatters build a fire in the empty lot to cook their dinner. A herd of carabao feed in this exclusive neighborhood. The contrasts are enormous.

Because we tend to interpret facts in light of our American, middle-class perspective, it is difficult to conceive how wide the gulf is between the "haves" and the "have-nots." I must admit that we lived in Asia for nearly a year before I could truly grasp the fact that most of the people in the world are not "middle class" but live out their lives at one end of the financial scale or the other, with the balance tipped firmly toward a hand-to-mouth existence. Oh, I had known this in my head. But it was not a reality to me.

During these two years God has allowed us to

form friendships at both ends of the gamut. We have eaten rice in a hand-built house with the mountain people, and prime rib at the Manila Intercontinental with the wealthy. And we have seen the deep needs of both. Best of all, we have seen with our own eyes that God can meet those needs.

There are four billion people in this world, and 56 percent of them live in Asia alone! I still have trouble visualizing them. Each one has his own needs, hopes, and dreams. Each one is an individual whose destiny is heaven or hell.

Lord, You said, "Lift up your eyes and look on the fields." Help us to look up from what we're doing. The harvest is people, and there are so many that they're blurry, Lord. Sharpen our vision.

Don't let our comfortable way of life blind us to their needs and their eternal destiny. Heal our near-sightedness. Let us see from Your perspective.

Open our eyes, Lord.
        Then, open our hearts . . .
                and our hands

        To give,
        To pray,
                To go . . .
                        To obey.